THE FELINE MUSE

THE FELINE MUSE

A Golden Quill Anthology

Edited by

EDWARD T. DELL, Jr.

Illustrations by Carol S. Pitman

THE GOLDEN QUILL PRESS
Publishers
Francestown   New Hampshire

Library of Congress Catalog Card Number 86-81933

ISBN 0-8233-0424-8

Acknowledgments of poems appearing in previous publications
appear in the BIOGRAPHIES section, starting on page 85.

Printed in the United States of America

DEDICATION
For Gus

CONTENTS

PARTING

INTRODUCTION

Cats abhor neutrality. They divide the world into antithetical groups who on the one hand, range in feelings from distaste to antipathy and on the other, from affection to adoration. In a survey about cats the "no opinion" category has no useful place.

Like many people I started life with a definitely uneasy attitude toward cats. We had one for a very short time until some doctor said it was making my sister sick, so we gave it away. One of my landladies had a charming cat, but he never succeeded in converting me.

The next stage in my education began when Heather, our eldest daughter began a concerted campaign for a pet, preferably a cat. Her parents, naturally, opposed the idea. The day she came home with a tiny creature in a shoebox, we reversed our position. The little mouse, it turned out, had already entered Valhalla some while ago, but the quality of Heather's determination clearly signalled ultimate defeat for our position.

Dandelion was a tiger-marked beauty who, even as a kitten, had the humor, wit and winsomeness that so often characterize these creatures. He survived just long enough to capture all our hearts, including mine, only to die in my arms a short while after an encounter with a passing automobile. One of fatherhood's hazards is the undertaker role for departed feline loved ones. Dandelion's death moved me out of the anti-cat camp into the other one.

Soon after, our youngest daughter picked the runt of the litter from a box in our family doctor's kitchen. Sara thought he was a good choice because he climbed over his mother to get out of the box.

At just this time we discovered T.S. Eliot's *Old Possum's Book of Practical Cats* and Robert Donat's reading of Eliot's delightful verses, set to Alan Rawsthorne's music. Under this influence, we named our new kitten Gus, or more formally, Asparagus. After Gus joined us my range of feline friends broadened steadily.

It is easy to go on at too great length about cats. My own appreciation for them rests on what I perceive as their essential independence of spirit, something Eliot refers to, I believe in his supposition that each cat has a secret, ineffable name known only to himself. The individuality and complexity of personal traits in each one and the seemingly infinite variety of feline personalities is, for me, one of the awe inspiring wonders of the created world.

A few years back when I took what seemed the ill-considered step of shouldering the responsibility for this publishing firm, the thought that I might have the pleasure of publishing a book of verse about cats seemed one of the genuinely attractive benefits.

I am most grateful to the contributors to this volume whose art gives us a renewed sense of the beauty and diversity of our friends who are feline.

Edward T. Dell, Jr.
Publisher

AT PLAY

AMBUSHED

A furry packet
but eight weeks old
unwanted guest
in my household.

He cried and cried
wanting sympathy
then turned and dashed
up the nearest tree.

He curled in my lap
began to purr
then decided to wash
his tawny fur.

A tiny pink nose
touched my hand
A soft little paw became
my heart's command.

SUE SNORF

LITTLE KITTEN

Little kitten, peacefully drowsing
after all your hunt and mousing
and your teasing, playful leaping,
do I wonder why you're sleeping?

All curled up with no concern,
with no thought to earn or learn,
with no clothes to soil and crease,
nary a care to fret your peace.

Little kitten, your rhythmic purr
is just as smooth as your soft fur;
with no worry for your keeping,
do I wonder why you're sleeping?

SARAH WINSTON

LITTLE BLACK PUSSY

Little black pussy,
You are so sweet,
With little round tummy
And soft little feet.

Little black pussy,
I love you so!
Don't you stay away
Wherever you go.

Little black pussy,
If you climb a tree,
Remember how you got there
And come back to me.

Little black pussy,
Come cuddle up tight.
God sent you to love me;
God bless you! Goodnight!

GRACE GARDNER

17

CONFIDENCE

Soft, wispy
Given to quick starts,
Climbable, chewable,
Side-frisking, un-
Catchable, a kitten is
Sudden tenderness
When asleep in the palm
Of a new-found friend.

FLORENCE ROME GARRETT

MISSY

Her paws are velvet now,
As she lies nodding in the morning sun;
Her whiskers twitch, her muscles ripple
As she begins her silent dreamer's run.
She's gold and white, this precious cat,
With eyes as clear and green as a wintry sea.
She puts her little head down
    When I ask her to,
        Because
  She knows it pleases me.

VIRGINIA WALMSLEY

FOR TIGGER AT CHRISTMAS

I remember how skinny you were when we first saw
    you:
enormous-eyed with a lost, starved look
glowing out of scrawny fur whose tigered markings
etched the fine bones of your skeleton.

They proudly showed us your mother, a Siamese
    showcat
who miaowed to be admitted at the front entrance
when we arrived.

She was beautiful . . . your father nameless . . .
"This is the kitten," they said with disgust,
"We think it's a male."

Never had I heard such loud purring when I held you
    up
for an instant . . .
fur soft as baby lambskin . . .

Now, you are nearly full grown
with a puckish personality and eyes like great jade
    marbles
set above owlish neckrings . . .

Secure in your birthright,
lord of our jungle
and four mewing hearts.

ELLIS OVESEN

THE FRIEND

PART-TIME CAT

When I had nothing left inside my house
but rawhide toys abandoned, I had thought
the wild birds near my window were enough.
They came and went, alive, anonymous,
asking little from me but their seed.
Then you appeared.

Our voids coincided—
the empty kennel in my heart
and changes never clear to me
in the pattern of your days
that brought you prowling
to the feeder in my yard.

From shouted scats to treats
to shelter on a rainy night
we went, myself protective
of feathers on the feeder, you
solitary, secret,
self-sufficient.

Timing your arrival to match mine,
meowing as you move across the drive,
you greet me seven nights of every ten.
I often wonder
when you don't appear
what other streets you work besides my own.

GERALD CLARKE

23

TAFFY
Mr. Erskine Caldwell's feline pet
speaks in praise of her chosen one.

You are my chosen one, or am I yours?
So unlike you are, a *nonpareil*
Is this the reason I want to be like you?
Or, better still, to be your second self?

Why should you look up, in that priceless print,
When all you hope the world will see is me,
A reborn Katy, Ade, Pearl and Bessie,
Ella Mae, Darling Jill, *et al.*

How you hold me there, so lovingly,
Happy, sweet Taffy, your second self reclining,
Purring, purring, no louder than a whisper,
For joy and peace abide in quietness.

Somewhere, there must be balm in Gilead—
That haloed brow, those selfless eyes,
Determined warrior's countenance
Charm me naturally to contemplate,

Upon something beautiful, something good—
Like social justice for castaway cats and kittens.
Since this is your *ultima Thule* for Sonny Clark,
We are champions for a common cause.

For this unity, I bow to you.
Dear chosen one, yours I'll be forever!
And now, I, Taffy, have one last request,
Since we have been through it all, together—

I have learned to trust, and I have been dreaming,
Dreaming of a little white marble Taj Mahal,
The color of my own cottony coat—
A little ivory mausoleum in Scottsdale

For memory's sake—after my nine lives are up—
And "I'll be satisfied with myself." Your Taffy.

ROSE E. BURCKHARDT

REPUTATION

By any ruse
or subterfuge
a fawning sigh
a servile lie
hungry nails
and waving tail
jaundiced eye
and piercing cry
nocturnal ways
halcyon days
with disdain imbued
by caress subdued

by strategy, flattery
    or definitive decree
jealousy, diversity
    or responsive degree
my kitty lends credence
    to her feline reputation.

SUE SNORF

26

ME AND MY THREE-LEGGED CAT

Me and my three-legged cat. . . .
We walk this farm together.

Through the garden patch
and by the fence. . .
She gimps worriedly
behind.
The sun burns low on the horizon
As we do the chores—
She gazes at me with
trusting eyes;
Following me in and out of doors. . .

The hens cluck low—
and the air is soft.
She knows she depends on me.

Me and my three-legged cat—
We walk this farm together.

MARY MOLYNEUX BOYER

SHAKESPEARE AFFICIONADO

My cat enjoys the classics read aloud,
Macbeth declaimed with fitting deep emotion
Just to an audience of her—no crowd
To dilute impact or distract devotion.
She sits and listens with her ears perked up,
Nor moves a muscle even when I stroke
Her silver fur; no pause to drink or sup,
For her gaze tells, the classics are no joke.
And so, on winter evenings by the fire,
I read of Hamlet and the ghosts he saw,
King Lear with all his anguish of desire,
Or Shylock, subject to such stringent law.
She finds it solacing, this weighty stuff,
And falls asleep when she has had enough.

ALICE MacKENZIE SWAIM

SMALL TALK, ANYONE?

I found myself quite lonely in a group of gals my age;
The conversation centered on grandchildren—every
   stage.
I had none; so I sat quite dumb—till, desperation-
   smitten,
I stopped the conversation by just mentioning my
   kitten.

I tried to change the subject: Recipes? United Nations?
They glanced at me with pity and began on
   operations.
I lacked in that department, too, but silenced them
   again
By giving them the details of my cat's Cesarean.

MYRNA HAIGHT

29

BEWITCHERY

TO A NIGHT TRAVELER

My car was scrutinized by you last night
In circuits right to left, and left to right.
Your dainty tracks, this frigid morning, show
Your explorations clearly in the snow.
Across the hood, along the windshield's base,
On top to either edge, your paw-prints trace
Your search for shelter from the icy air.
I wish you could have found a haven there,
An entry, whisker-wide, to let you be
Secure against last night's inclemency.
It would have pleased my fancy had your quest
Permitted me to have a cat as guest.
Excuse the constant dismal guard I keep;
I hope you found a warm, dry place to sleep.

IRENE WARSAW

NONPAREIL

It is written that in Arabia,
Prophet Mohammed sheltered
A little white kitten, his pet.
So mindful was he for her safety,
That once when he spoke from the great
Minaret in Mecca,
He found his beloved asleep
In a sleeve of his canonical robe.
Since to summon men to prayer,
He must wear the sacred gown,
He cut off the sleeve,
  so kitty could breathe
   and d-r-e-a-m,
SANS PEUR ET SANS
  REPROCHE

       ROSE E. BURCKHARDT

THE SIGNIFICANCE OF GOOD CARRIAGE

Egyptian cats were deified
And mummified and golden-eyed.
Slinky slim and long of face
They look today as they did when
The gods were cognizant of place.
In temples that they dignified
Despite the honor paid to them
These traitors spurned the human race,
And will again.

VIRGINIA M. STETSER

THE SLEEPING CAT

I watch you while you sleep
your head tucked
under your paw. . .

Such serenity should
come to humans—

perfect creature!
with steady breathing
and
white whiskers
arching
softly.

MARY MOLYNEUX BOYER

TO DARCY, AN INDOMITABLE SPHINX

Reincarnation of the mysteries
Of ancient Egypt and the templed Nile,
She licks her paws, completely at her ease,
And watches me with Mona Lisa smile.
Seductive, subtle, Cleopatra-smug,
With very obvious yawn and smothered purr,
Relaxed in languor on the Persian rug,
She makes me feel too, too inferior.
So with sly blandishments, I try to woo
The favors of this so inscrutable
Small cat, with some ambrosial fishy brew
That she may find quite irresistible.
How well she knows that in her silken paw
Lies love to grant or favor to withdraw.

ALICE MacKENZIE SWAIM

SINISTRAL

The cat you noted — the one
who chooses damp corners of the basement,
long unlit passages and only
the occasional company of a stray
person for scraps of food,
the chance to fix his cross
look upon the memory

You called him something of an outlaw —
dignified the odd lurking presence
at the foot of the basement stair
discomfited, leering for something
yet darting off at first signs of warmth

The fix on that bi-colored orange face,
black breaking between
his eyes in jagged lines
that run up/down
bissecting the neat wedge-shaped
head into opposing hemispheres

Just once I saw him sunlit
on a woman's lap
the black/orange less remarkable
in daylight than in cellar shadow

Late one night — spotting him
cornered in darkness I remarked to you:
He really wants nothing
from humanity or his own kind

Do you suppose he was never
properly suckled, nosed out
from mother-care by stronger
brothers and sisters?

Your answer, spat with conviction:
No! It was too much! Too much
attention — fussing! All of that!

And in silence we
climbed the stair.

NATALE SAFIR

SIMPLE FEATS

Patrolling
a narrow margin
in simple feats
of precision
the furred knobs
of her feet
in total
self possession

It is not enough
to step over and
around the milkglass jar,
lacquer tray
and silver bracelet

Wisdom aligns
that complex bit
of spine that allows
nothing
to get in her way

NATALE SAFIR

40

TO A BEWITCHING CAT

Those amber eyes veil mystery;
That velvet coat sheathes lithesome grace.
Egypt ascribes you deity;
Your haunt, the home and marketplace.

That velvet coat sheathes lithesome grace.
You bask before my vestal fire;
Your haunt, the home and marketplace.
My homage grants your heart's desire.

You bask before my vestal fire,
Triumphant in supreme content.
My homage grants your Heart's desire;
Accept my humble blandishment.

Mouser, who stalks for stealthy gain,
Egypt ascribes you deity.
Though purrs deny a cruel disdain,
Those amber eyes veil mystery.

HELEN FOUNTAIN

41

TO A CELEBRITY NAMED MORRIS

-1-

Elusive creature, with a languid grace,
You bask in warmth before an open fire.
Inscrutability, which masks your face,
Reflects the Buddha. Why should we admire
Your independence when you oft require
Attention? Mews may vocalize the need
Of bed and board to satisfy your breed.

-2-

In daylight hours, your attitude is meek;
Composure offers us a purring mood,
Yet you can hiss when in a frenzied pique,
As rivals lurk or steal your dish of food;
In fact, some protestations grow quite rude.
Courtship by moonlight brings a serenade
Disturbing weary neighbors who upbraid.

-3-

While passion may disrupt the calm, your eyes
Express a burning ardor as you sing
In alleys. Love becomes a cruel surprise,
For cat fights often leave their brutal sting
From such encounters. Frequent battles bring
Those bloody wounds with scraps of fur about.
Bold lover, have you lost the victor's clout?

-4-

Domestic Shorthair, Tortoise Shell, Maltese,
Angora, Manx, and Persian, those proud winners
Must join with the exotic Siamese;
They speak a common tongue who beg for dinners,
While many gorge all day, the greedy sinners.
Some born as pedigreed aristocrats
May prove no smarter than the alley cats.

-5-

John Masefield has admired cat's cunning charm.
His photograph, a winsome shot, displays
A friendly puss that lies upon his arm.
It shares a blessing, comforts lonely days
With gentle purrs, contented sounds of praise.
Time keeps this treasured moment; true affection
Held by the lens for happy recollection.

-6-

"Old Possum," T. S. Eliot, describes
Those many cats. Such literary fame
Marks human traits in their prolific tribes.
He lauds diversity and would acclaim
The certain one who bears a secret name,
That only cat, itself, might ever know
But not divulge to either friend or foe.

Egyptian goddess, Pasht, has wielded power
In temples where her idol gained esteem,
Enthralling worshipers, who by the hour
Attended rituals. Cats dined on cream,
Because they rid the land of rats. Their theme
Resounded from the choir beside an altar;
Priests venerated Pasht with feline Psalter.

Your ancestors were known as harmful creatures,
Consigned by many folks to depths of hell.
Their lives were judged by superstitious preachers,
Who claimed that felines brought an evil spell;
While Satan's art was taught by wicked teachers,
Condemned as witches damned by divination.
Were cats the means of their communication?

Intrepid cat, though you were once despised,
That competence in catching rats who thieved,
Restored prestige. Though never idolized
In western countries, you have been relieved
From torture. Those who cherished cats were grieved
When you were victimized by harsh abuse;
Thus wiser generations called a truce.

Impersonation proves dramatic skill.
Though you lack words, my friend, you might express
Soliloquies with merit. You fulfill
Commercial roles with an urbane finesse,
For TV fans applaud you. We confess
Your craftiness continues, but admit
You play the lead, belovéd hypocrite.

HELEN FOUNTAIN

EVA PRES DUBUQUE

The soft shoe dancer
in my back yard owns it all,
domain diva, tigress
of the hunt, avian
equalizer.

She works mysteries
locked down in her broad head,
territorial scents defiled,
paths of star crossed
hunters

gridding her scheme
of things; overhead the stars
ache in their assessment
of her three point world,
three paws down, one
reaching slowly
in easy air

like some boy, fifteen,
his throat dry, afraid to breathe,
praying one last prayer,
reaches through soft air
for a breast

and a girl, fifteen,
liquid, mouth and heart ajar,
body tight in a ring of self,
waits the slow hand,
the quick lover.

My cat's name is
of no consequence.

THOMAS F. SHEEHAN

THE EYES

Deep in the dark jungle, Baby,
This tiger lies,
A contagious hungry quiet
Upon his face,
Gathered in a ferny silence,
His smouldering gaze
Waiting for the careless moment
When, fawn-doe wise,
My strayed heart, exploring shyly
Those jungle ways,
Passes, looks in his direction,
And locks her eyes
With the final meaning of their
Deceptive peace.

If she ever once glances at
The way he lies
Crouched on the cool sinking mosses
And hoards his gaze,
She'll be going shortly, Baby,
Those jungle ways,
Running down their green dark alleys
To feed her eyes
On that smouldering slow hunger,
And your lost voice,

Calling, calling, will not reach her
For all the noise
Of the jungle cats' terrific
Wails and cries.

JOHN MOFFITT

FIGURE IN FIRELIGHT

The vast of life deceives—
                                        comprises
ghastly compromises:
  ladies' wraps of unborn lamb/
  foie gras/ *gold and diamonds*
  torn by blacklunged men and boys
  from suburbias of Hades/
  shackled lobsters boiled alive...

How else this magic carpet
but from a half-starved child?
wide-eyed   weary   wan—
who else with such desperate delight
would weave
my Siamese stretched out
across the warp of firelight
reflected on this hearthrug
wrought in Ispahan?

RAYMOND HENRI

SIAMESE AMONG THE IRISES
(For Thai)

Lanceolate leaves clash above him.

Mindful of his heritage
Thai maintains sheathed
his bluesteel scimitar eyes
just visible
within black velvet scabbards—
ignores
the silent skirmish,
parades
with
       single
            footed
dignity
and scorns
thrust and parry
of green swords.

RAYMOND HENRI

RITE OF SPRING

For a cat released from winter's grip
into the stunning freshness of green air
there's need to shrink a winter's waiting
into burst of action. Oh rapturous exercise!

to destroy a peacock.
                    To surprise him
at the summit of conceit, stretched
upper coverts locked aquiver
in paralysis of passion.

                    To claw
and tear away the blue-green feather eyes,
set them afloat in vortices of dust—
to hack the great erectile train into
a tousled rick of gold and glaucous fragments.

As ceremony's coda:
to snap the shimmering imbrication of
his neck and topple crown into the dirt.

Oh rapturous exercise for claws fed up
with winter shrews, alike alive or dead.

RAYMOND HENRI

WHO'S BOSS

REQUIES-CAT

Whatever became of the A & P cat,
The store-window cat, who so pompously sat
Between apple and pear, with superior stare?

He just vanished, like that.
Did someone say "Scat?"

FRANCES E. HOLMES

CAT'S REPERTOIRE
(A most inelegant explanation)

Meh, meh, meh
    There are birds and mice outside
    Such interests ought not be denied
Meowów, meowów, meowów
    Sometimes I am quite lonely
    I'm looking for playmates only
Owwów, owwów, owwów
    I may be on a mating prowl
    Reason enough for my caterwaul
Psst, psst, psst
    I'm having now a junior spat
    With our neighbor's snooty Persian cat
Oww, oww, oww
    But now I'm in a frightful jam
    Swaying dizzily in a tree I am
Meów, meów, meów
    Innocently at my master's door
    Pleading, "May I come in once more?"
Púrrez, púrrez, púrrez
    I'll curl up now for a little nap
    Content I'll sleep in Suzy's lap.

SUE SNORF

PURRFECT LADY

I fell in love with a lady
Who thought her word was law,
From the slightest flick of a plumy tail
To the stamp of imperious paw,

Or a yawn of utter boredom,
A lick at immaculate fur,
And when all was to her liking,
A condescending purr.

I hadn't the heart to tell her,
Being so deeply smitten,
That in the eyes of the rest of the world,
She was merely a Persian kitten!

ALICE MacKENZIE SWAIM

THE CAT

Long-haired and black as shadow
the cat comes to drive
a pad of yellow foolscap
and a ballpoint pen out

of the Inhabitant's hands for
it is time again to
handle the palpable dark not
to compose to write about

the loom and shuttle of
shadow moving mechanically across clock
faces but to pass hands
lightly down the pelt of

smooth moments look you no
harm is meant by this
passage it is just that
things were meant to be

this way the waiting the
soft animal with sharp teeth
and claws sheathed lurking in
corners will come out to

be stroked and enjoyed for
it is lethal but sensual
as well and it means
no particular ill the hour

for striking has not arrived
it is not the enemy
but a familiar of houses
a domestic that keeps accounts.

LEWIS TURCO

MURGATROYD

Whenever we would open, there he stood,
With the supreme authority of need:
The face with pansy markings, eyes alight;
The body young, as meager as a bird's
Under the lusterless neglected fur.

Our cat confronted him, the Amazon,
Disdainful princess, nourished and secure,
Swinging her paw at the intruder there;
He quivered, but continued hovering
As if it were impossible to fail.

Our guilt, intolerable, weighed us down:
After three days, a saucerful of milk;
Complete capitulation, gates ajar
To grooming and a cushion and our love.
These were his right; he never questioned it.

CELESTE TURNER WRIGHT

MURPHY

Sleeping in my easy chair
Who would ever guess,
He's the little fellow
That makes the house a mess.

He snags my lacy curtains
He spills his milk and food,
While I am hoping daily
He'll soon become subdued.

He races up and down the stairs
And all around each room.
Investigating everything
He tries to fight the broom.

Although I scold him loudly
He's not afraid of me—
Today I'm in a state of shock
To find that he's a she!

JOSEPHINE B. MORETTI

61

CAT

8 a.m. the swift click
of a lock closing
shorts her daylight
into dark

Metallic sonar saucers
her bewildered eyes
tilt to catch
any chance ray

Into the hair
of the flokati rug
she curls watching
nothing happen,
waits for the windowsill plant
to shift for its light,
an occasional wheeze
from the water faucet,
sizzle and hiss
of radiators

Solar night sleeps
across her long afternoon

Does she know
it will end with the small tick
of a key pressing the talon
to shoot the bolt open,
her green eyes fired to attention?

Then fur will waft,
she'll spin metal fasteners
across hardwood,
leap to the sigh and creak
of knobs turning,
study silver water splatter
the bathtub or swipe
at an earwig scurrying, when

She will mewl
and be heard, push her nose
against sleeve or shin,
rise to the touch of flesh
exciting her back

NATALE SAFIR

PRINCESS OF ILLOGIC

She acts as if she were on high,
looking down on me,
a colorless form intersecting her world:
a robot to feed her, open the door.

Her arousing yawn arches
a little teeth-edged cavern of pink,
a tongue tipped like a rose petal—
so soft when she licks my hand.

She purrs only when I—her slave—
keep her in the mood: a balm
of milk, fish, bits of crisp, lean bacon,
a saunter across the grand piano.

In theory I'm her master, yet
why do I put up with her—
with that periodical brash yowling—
let her reverse textbook logic?

A pet, of course, does usurp seductively,
but her eyes do more:
green marbles with black slants
into ancient time linking her

to me, to the present of wonder
as her sable fur with a button of white
sheds to regain its sheen,
her claws keen for big game.

CHARLES CLINE

t

CAT SCAN

The cat
slides around the room,
knows something about me,
threatens to tell.
Wears secrets
in her eyes subtle
as jewels.

I swear she is
old as fear,
knows hair rise
and spine curve
is simple talk.

Plods about on paws
silent as roots.
I think she dreams
a chase in high grass,
recognition of game,
that other life
she found in my eyes.

THOMAS F. SHEEHAN

MIDDLE TIME

THE NEW CAT

This place seems to attract them—
Up in the shack there's
an old tiger tom...
wild and pretty...
He thinks he has a home.

Out on the edge of our
property
a calico appeared—
soft furred
and
rubbing affectionate.

She feels welcome too...
She sits on my
woodpile
and surveys—
the possibilities . . .

MARY MOLYNEUX BOYER

FOR DOMINO, A GOOD NEIGHBOR

He bears himself as conscious of his worth,
A Senior Citizen of fifteen years;
Friendly to all, subservient to none,
He savors life with nose and ears and eyes
In good repair, so that a luckless bird
Is sometimes pounced on in the dewy grass.

Nature chose black and white in making him,
And lavished special care upon his paws
Which show a tasteful balance of both hues.

He finds our porch entirely to his taste,
Shady and safe, complete with special chair
For summer nights or cat-naps around noon.
But when the dog days come with stifling heat
He spreads his furry length upon the planks,
Lifts his hind legs to let a chance breeze through,
Steadies his paws against the balustrade
And sinks in deepest dreams. Dear Domino,
May they be soft and clawless, rich with fish.

WINIFRED RAWLINS

DAISY UP A TREE

Over the housetops
In the highest pine
A yellow, black, white
Spot faces the wrong way
For coming down. Elderly
But still lithe, Daisy
Awaits a signal—I,
Whose past performance
Is unimpeachable, set
Myself, call loud and firm,
It's all right, Daisy
Come down, Now.

She turns, somehow,
Puts down one back leg
Another leg, looks down
Backward, cringes—
You can make it, Daisy.
From the highest tree
Ever she hangs in love,
Backing, slowly backing
Down finally to a jumping
Position, to a well executed
Leap, to a brief rather haughty
Reunion with her quaking servant.

FLORENCE ROME GARRETT

71

A CAT DISTURBED

A cat
disturbed from sleep
spins three, four circled
around his tail
to scythe and trample down
nettle dreams into a clover pallet
on which he then resumes
his nap.

RAYMOND HENRI

PARTING

THE ACCIDENT

Crow-black cat curiously
Sprawled at rest right
Where the curbstone curves,
Your legs stretched grandly
Straight, just as often
Before a charmed hearth
Well-fed drowsy cats
Bask: that glossy coat
Invites the hand, its every
Sparkling hair in place,
No telltale stain or shudder
Shown—if only your round
Arrested eyes, staring,
Staring into a bottomless
Something, didn't trancedly
Warn a tempted watcher
That your unmoving pose is
More final than its angles
Reveal, your fascinated
Gaze more unguessable
Than that you turned perhaps
Last evening on your watching
Master as, prophetic,
You lay by the charmed hearth,
Your legs stretched grandly
Straight, your round yellow
Eyes staring, staring.

JOHN MOFFITT

75

ELEGY FOR A BLUE-EYED SIAMESE

Flow like quicksilver
into that great night
you desperately wanted to explore.
Walk delicately
on padded velvet feet,
not disarranging one least grain of dust
along leaf-hidden trails.
Into the darkness
leap with that eagerness
you hunted butterflies,
or chased stray leaves that blew across
the landscapes of your kittenhood.
Eyes glowing with old dreams, unrealized,
leap boldly through the open door of now,
your whiskers trembling with anticipation.
Though sorrowing, I would not drag you back
from this great final exploration.

ALICE MacKENZIE SWAIM

THAI

Even in death beautiful—
long pointed ears
alert
as if to sound of trumpets
none ever hears.

RAYMOND HENRI

THE DAY AFTER

It was the day after
by the time you told me.
By the time you told me
Public Works had flung
her by the river
for landfill.

You sat at my bedside
telling me
that you did not know
though her white fur
twitched
in your rear mirror
like a nerve
and you did not
stop to see.

But I saw. I knew.

But all morning
I raked the street
calling her calling her
knowing I would find
no body
to wrap in my arms
weep my face
in her dead fur.

All morning calling her
seeing your brown car
breaking my cat
the whole story
between us breaking
in pieces all over
the wet road.

NATALE SAFIR

THROUGH EMPTY ROOMS

I

When thermometer red shrinks
and snow squalls obscure
our winter scene
Kinetic excitement comes prancing,
preens sparks from his fur
from his dancing paws;
Leaps to the windowsill become
wild arcs—this morning he almost
made it to the steps . . .
The cardinal sings over him,
crimson as the pool
in which he lies.
The bluejay will never scream at him
again from his favorite tree
in challenge.

II

Already we assess our loss: furry knuckles
rap at the basement door, lithe demand
weaves a wistful plea
Of hunger round our ankles; curious eyes
answer our silent call, peer at us
from the stair
Now only curious air. A strange sound
in the night—a question,
lingering, as we go

Into a room and see bare window shelf,
   his mat now put away . . . Still
      we leap to answer
The assault upon the screen,
   open the door to find
      only the wind.

CECILIA PARSONS MILLER

IN HER NINETEENTH YEAR

I sat beside her on the back-porch steps
and groomed her one last time.
Eyes bright with pain,
she humped to meet the brush strokes as before,
but had no strength to purr.

She'd always hated visits to the vet.
This final trip we'd put off far too long,
knowing its portent. Lifting her, he said,
"There's not much left of her," and we agreed.
By then she had become
a fragile skeleton in sagging fur,
less heavy than this paper in my hand,
that reads: "Humane destruction and disposal—
one old cat."

MYRNA HAIGHT

BIOGRAPHIES and ACKNOWLEDGEMENTS

BIOGRAPHIES and ACKNOWLEDGEMENTS

Mary Molyneux Boyer was born in northern Wisconsin in 1942. When quite young she moved with her family to the foothills of the Appalachians in Pennsylvania where she spent most of her childhood. She has published poems in *Encore, The National Poetry Journal,* and *Peninsular Poets.* Her small volume of poems *Pale Ponies* appeared in 1983. She is at work on a small autobiography *The Wings of a Turtledove.*

"Me and My Three-Legged Cat" and "The New Cat"
  The National Poetry Journal

Rose E. Burckhardt an enthusiastic poet, artist and world traveler, has published *The Cantatrice* (GQP, 1979) and *The Cantatrice II* (GQP, 1984). A retired teacher and college professor, she lives in Bourbonnais, Illinois, an area she characterizes as ideal, "...pervaded as it is by a benevolent spirit."

Gerald Clarke has published two volumes of poetry *Airling* (GQP, 1977) and *McGregor School* (GQP, 1980) and contributed poems to numerous magazines. A career teacher, he now lives near Arizona's Sonoran desert where "...he sees in every season that fragility and tenacity of life his poems celebrate."

"Part-Time Cat" Won honorable mention in *Negative Capability*'s Eve of St. Agnes contest (Vol III, No. 1, 1982). The periodical publishes poetry, translation and fiction in Mobile, Alabama.

Charles Cline is professor of English and poet-in-residence at Kellog Community College in Michigan. His books include *Crossing the Ohio* (GQP, 1976), *Questions for the Snow* (GQP, 1979) and a chapbook, *Ultima Thule*. He is a 1986 literary competition winner in the World Institute of Achievement.

"Princess of Illogic"
   Poet, (27 April 1986).

Helen Fountain a retired teacher, has won numerous awards for her poetry. Her three volumes include *Star Quest* (1967), *A Cage of Birds* (GQP, 1970) and *In A Teahouse* (GQP, 1979). A charter Fellow in The International Academy of Poets, she is also listed in *Who's Who of American Women*.

"To a Celebrity Named Morris"
   Second Award, The World Order of Narrative Poets.
"To a Bewitching Cat"
   In a Teahouse (GQP, 1979)

Grace Howard Gardner is a native of Hartford, Connecticut. Having earned her Master of Arts from Yale she has devoted a lifetime to teaching and writing for young children. The children's corner of North Haven's Ridge Road library is named in her honor. She is author of numerous books of poetry for the young.

"Little Black Pussy"
   Teacher Tells More Tales (1956)

Florence Rome Garrett resides in Bridgewater, Connecticut. Her books include *Edge of Day* (1954), *More Than the Quiet Pond* (GQP, 1969), *On the Hill* (1977), *The Mill and Us* (1978), *Japanese Sketches* (1980) and *Bridgewater Morning* (1986). She is listed in *Who's Who of American Women*, is a Fellow of the International Academy of Poets and a Member and Awards recipient of the National League of American Pen Women.

Myrna Haight, born and raised in Iowa, received her B.A. from that state's University and taught English and Art in South Dakota for 35 years. A member of the National League of American Pen Women, her poems have been published in numerous periodicals and have won many awards. *Shadow Flecked Roads* (GQP, 1981) is her most recent book of poetry.

"In Her Nineteenth Year" and "Small Talk, Anyone"
  Shadow Flecked Roads (GQP, 1981).

Raymond Henri—Regrettably, no biography available.

"Figure in Firelight"
  Dispatches from the Fields (by author)

Frances E. Holmes—Regrettably, no biography available.

"Resquies-Cat"
  The Troubadour Vermont Poetry Society magazine, (Spring 1975)

Cecelia Parsons Miller, who resides in Lemoyne, Pennsylvania, has given her life to poetry, having published nine volumes, the latest two being *Shadows and Light* (1983) and *Out-Chasing Tradition* (1984). She has been most active in the National Federation of State Poetry Societies having been its first president in 1959, and founder and first editor of its newsletter *Strophes*. She was editor and publisher of *Prize Poems* 1958-70, 1975-76, and 1979-85.

"Through Empty Rooms"
  Encore and *Cyclo-Flame* annual 1972

John Moffit, poetry editor of *America* magazine, is the author, in addition to his five volumes of poetry, of *Journey to Gorakhpur: An Encounter With Christ Beyond Christianity* and *The Road to Now: Claiming Our Spiritual Birthright* which are the fruit of his previous long experience as a Hindu monk. A graduate of Princeton, he was born at Harrisburg, Pennsylvania in 1908.

"The Accident"
  The Living Seed (New York: Harcourt, Brace & World, 1962)

Josephine Moretti has been writing poems for over fifty years. While she began with serious verse, she turned to the lighter side some twenty years ago. The change is clearly evident in her two books *Home Is Where...* (GQP, 1974) and *Love Is Where...* (GQP, 1982). In her home town of Jenkintown, Pennsylvania she is known as *The Poem Lady*.

"Murphy"
  Love Is Where. . . (GQP, 1982)

Ellis Ovesen, author of ten volumes of poetry, three of which, *A Book of Praises* (1977), *The Green Madonna* (1984) and *The Wing-Brush* (1986), were published by Golden Quill Press, resides in Los Altos, California. Her wide-ranging talents include poetry, songs, dance, prophecy, and abstract symbolist painting. She is listed in *Who's Who of American Women* and *World Who's Who of Women*, Cambridge, England.

"For Tigger at Christmas"
  Haloed Paths (Prairie Poet Books, Charleston, IL 1973)
  A Book of Praises (GQP, 1977)

Winifred Rawlins born in 1907 in London, she now lives in Moylan, Pennsylvania where she has been a peace activist, farm worker, taught music, worked with refugees and directed retirement homes. Of her eight collections of published poetry, four were published by Golden Quill Press. Her poems have been widely published including appearances in *Best Poems of 1964*.

Natale Safir is the author of *Moving Into Seasons* (GQP, 1981). Her recent work has appeared in many periodicals including *Pivot Images, Croton Review,* and *Madison Review*. She directs The Pomegranite Series of Writers and Readers and teaches poetry writing workshops in Hastings-on-Hudson, New York.

"Sinistral" and "The Day After"
  Moving Into Seasons (GQP, 1981)

Thomas F. Sheehan lives in Saugus, Massachusetts where he is a busy poet, his work having appeared in *Cutbank Long Pond Review, Pembroke Images, Indiana Review, Alaska Review, Spitball, Blue Buildings, Kansas Quarterly,* and *Ceilidh*. His books include *Ah, Devon Unbowed* (GQP, 1979) and *The Saugus Book* (GQP, 1984).

"Cat Scan"
  Cape Rock, 1981

Sue Snorf, born in Clay Township near Verona, Ohio in 1896, she was educated at Miami University, Oxford, Ohio and took her M.A. at Ohio State. She taught at a number of posts, the longest at Wilbur Wright High School from which she retired after 47 years of service. She has traveled extensively and is the author of *Stillwater Valley* (GQP, 1985).

Virginia Masland Stetser mother of five and a graduate of Wilson College includes teaching, editing, publishing and volunteer work among her activities. Author of four books including *African Palette* (GQP, 1979), she has traveled extensively with her architect husband. Many of her poems were inspired by her travels.

"The Significance of Good Carriage" is reprinted with the permission of *Poetry Society of America Bulletin*.

Alice Mackenzie Swaim lives in Harrisburg, Pennsylvania where poetry is her prime interest. Author of 14 books, numerous articles and over 7,000 poems, she is active in the Poetry Society of America and has been an active participant in the affairs of state poetry societies of California, Kentucky, New Hampshire and Pennsylvania as well as the National Federation of State Poetry Societies. Her three Golden Quill volumes include *Beyond My Catnip Garden* (1970), *Gentle Dragon* (1962) and *Out of Darkness* (1962).

"Elegy for a Blue-Eyed Siamese" (On program of the National Cat Show, Baton Rouge, LA 1983)

Lewis Turco directs the Program for Writing Arts at the State University of New York at Oswego. His *The Compleat Melancholick* (Bieler Press) appeared in 1985. Both his books of criticism, *Visions and Revisions of American Poetry* (University of Arkansas Press) and *The New Book of Forms* (University Press of New England), were published in 1986. His *First Poems* was published by Golden Quill Press in 1960.

"The Cat" Reprinted from *The Inhabitant*, Northampton, MA (Despa Press 1970). All rights reserved by Mathom Press Enterprises, Box 362, Oswego NY 13126.

Virginia Walmsley was born in Findlay, Ohio and educated at Malone College. A mother of two she is also a musician, a writer and homemaker. When not traveling, reading, or caring for her two much loved cats she visits her one grandchild. Her poem "Missy" has become a memorial as Missy died shortly after her poem was written.

Irene Warsaw is a native of Michigan where she has lived and worked for most of her life. Recently retired from a career as a specialist in trusts and estates, she devotes her time to her deep interest in poetry as a judge, lecturer and guest speaker. Her poetry, especially in her two volumes from Golden Quill, *A Word In Edgewise* (1964) and *Warily We Roll Along* (1979), examines the incongrous side of life with insight and glee. She is a member of the National League of Pen Women and Detroit Women Writers.

"To a Night Traveler" Reprinted with the permission of The McCall Publishing Company. Published in *McCall's*, February, 1982.

Sarah Winston is a busy and successful author of both poetry and prose living in Havertown, Pennsylvania. Her books include *V-Mail: Letters of a World War II Combat Medic* (Algonquin 1985), *Not Yet Spring* (GQP, 1976), *Everything Happens for the Best* (A.S. Barnes, 1970), *Our Son, Ken* (Dell, 1970), and *And Always Tomorrow* (Holt, 1963).

"Little Kitten"
  Not Yet Spring (GQP, 1976)

Celeste Turner Wright is *emeritus* Professor of English at the University of California, Davis. Her collection *A Sense of Place* (GQP) won a medal from San Francisco's Commonwealth Club as "...one of the four best books published by California authors in 1973." Dr. Wright is also author of *Seasoned Timber* (GQP, 1977).

"Murgatroyd"
A Sense of Place (GQP, 1973)

GQP refers to THE GOLDEN QUILL PRESS

92